THE ADVANCED CRAIGSLIST RESELLER GUIDE

How to Make Extra Money or Create a Side Income By Reselling On Craigslist

Steve Johnson

Contents

Introduction

These days, there are many ways in which to make a profit if you look hard enough. Some of these avenues might not seem obvious at first, but once you do your research and think a little outside of the box, you'll be surprised at some of the ways you can make cash for whatever endeavor you're focusing on.

The bottom line is that life can be expensive, and with increasing prices and static wages, more and more people are choosing to find sidelines to make extra cash. This can be a substantial amount, or perhaps just a little extra cash and here and there. Regardless of the amount, having a profitable sideline can be a useful method for lining a bank account in hard economic times.

This book is going to talk about one very successful and quite easy way to make cash, once you know the ins and outs and the general basics.

Have you heard of Craigslist?

Craigslist is a hugely popular auction selling website, which allows people to sell their unwanted items locally, without having to worry about the problems associated with shipping and sending items cross country, or even internationally. There are many auction reselling sites out there, and even pages and boards on social media sites, such as Facebook. Whilst these are useful, there are some downsides associated with selling on eBay especially - namely fees.

In many ways, Craigslist is a little like eBay, but without the fees and without the hassle. For this reason, many people are using Craigslist as a way to make extra cash, and not just for selling items they don't want. You do not need to pay fees when you sell something on Craigslist, but you do on eBay, and the more you sell the item for, the higher the fees. You also don't need to box up the item and ship it to the person's address, never sure if it has actually arrived in one piece. Craigslist is a local site, and therefore collections are done in person, either from a house (not the most recommended option) or form a mutually convenient pickup point. From a safety point of view, mutual public pick up points are best.

How can you make cash by reselling items on this popular selling site? This book is going to answer that exact question and show you how to do it from scratch. By the end of this book, you'll be ready and excited to get started on your own reselling business. Whilst profits might not come to you in abundance straight away, with a little time building up your reselling business, you'll find more gains coming your way.

What is Reselling?

Reselling on Craigslist can be done in two distinct ways.

- Firstly, you run a business selling items to buyers, sourcing your items from outside businesses, e.g. trade manufacturers or other auction sites. You can choose to have a stock which you sell, or you can source as and when a sale takes place. This is a more difficult way to resell items on Craigslist.

- Secondly, you purchase an item from Craigslist and sell it on for a higher price. This option is the best way to get started with reselling, and sourcing out bargains will no doubt become an addiction!

Both options involve finding a niche which has demand. For instance, perhaps in your local area, you find that cellphone accessories sell very well. In this case, you would purchase cellphone cases for a low price and you would sell them on for a higher cost, making a profit in the process. You can then grow your business by branching out to other associated items, such as laptop accessories, phone chargers, etc. Whilst you're probably never going to become a millionaire from reselling on Craigslist, you can certainly make a tidy profit every month.

How much? You could make between $300 - 700 per month. That's the same amount as a part-time job! For that reason, we're going to class reselling on Craigslist as a passive income method, i.e. you're making money with not much effort, and you could even do it on the side, alongside your regular full time or another part-time job.

How This Book Will Help You

This book is a from scratch guide on how to become a quality reseller on Craigslist. There is more to this subject than you will first realize, and it's very similar to starting your own business.

To stop your reselling becoming a hindrance to the rest of your life, e.g. encroaching on your own time or your primary job, you need to arrange your time and plan everything carefully. If you can do this, you will find that reselling on Craigslist will bring you profits with little effort, and it could even become an enjoyable hobby!

We will take about what it takes to become a reseller, the pros and cons, how to arrange your time, and how to find a product which sells well. At the end of the book, you will also find a bonus chapter. This chapter is an interview with a computer hardware reseller who has made a tidy profit from reselling on Craigslist. This shows you just how much of a reality this all can be, and you'll also be able to find out useful information, with insider hints and tips.

So, enough procrastination, let's get started on learning more about reselling on Craigslist, before diving into the specifics.

Chapter 1: Why do You Want to be a Reseller on Craigslist?

First things first, why should you become a reseller on Craigslist? It's no good starting something if you're not sure what is in it for you! You also need to have a clear view of what reselling is, and what it is going to involve.

Craigslist reselling isn't a difficult process once you know what your niche area is going to be. The difficulty comes in when you are identifying what you are going to sell and how you're going to sell it. You need to choose a product, or a range of products, which you are sure has a demand. For instance, purchasing a range of antiques and expecting to sell them in an area which is not so affluent for a high price is unrealistic. On the other hand, if you live in an area which has a high amount of teenagers or youngsters, then the cell phone accessory route is more than likely going to bring you profits.

It's about knowing your area, knowing the people who live there, and understanding what they like and don't like. You also need to make sure that you don't choose prices which are far too high. If you can do your research and work all of this out before you begin, you'll find your business flourishes quite quickly. On the other hand, if you jump in feet first, you're likely to stumble a few times before you find your feet.

Research and planning are key!

The Benefits of Reselling on Craigslist

In order to pursue something, you need to know you're going to benefit from it! We don't work for anything, and whilst Craigslist reselling isn't a particularly in-depth or difficult process, it still takes time and effort to some degree.

Let's explore the main benefits of reselling on Craigslist.

Extra Income

Let's start with the most obvious of reasons. Reselling items on Craigslist can bring extra cash your way. The more you sell, the more money you make, and the more you learn about the reselling process, the more accurate you will become on your pricing. A little later in this book, we're going to talk about tips to maximize your sales, and therefore bring extra cash and exposure your way. The more people you reach, the more chances you have of making cash!

The first time you make a sale on Craigslist, it's likely to be a low amount, however, you need to cast your net quite wide at first. If you can do this, and if you can be persistent, you will notice greater gains.

Many people choose to use reselling on Craigslist as a passive income method. This is something you can do on the side, in your spare time, which doesn't take up a huge amount of your time after the initial set up stage. Other possible passive income methods include renting out a home you own, and receiving rental payments from tenants every month, dabbling in the stock market, affiliate marketing through blogging, and writing a book and selling it for royalties. None of these methods have no effort involved, and the first set up process will take time, but after that, they basically run themselves.

Whilst Craigslist reselling isn't completely hands-off, it does take minimal time once you manage to streamline your own process and create a business flow which suits your time and your needs.

You Meet a Range of People

The good thing about Craigslist is that it isn't impersonal, e.g. you get to actually meet the person you're selling to, and you have communication with them over the phone or via email. This means you're going to inevitably meet people you don't want to, of course, but it also means you get to meet new people who you might click with too. You never know, you could meet a new friend through your reselling endeavors!

We touched upon safety a little earlier on, and because Craigslist reselling hinges on in-person meetings to pass the item over and transfer the money, you do have to be more careful than you would be if you were using a site like eBay. The lack of time spent parceling up items and sending them to an address is at the expense of your time, i.e. you need to go and meet the person.

You should always ensure that you meet in the day time, in a public place, and that you don't arrange for anyone to pick items up from your home address, or that you go to an address you do not know. Of course, there are going to be times when at-home pickups can't be avoided, e.g. for large items. In this case, never go alone, and never be home alone when the person visits. Simply use your common sense and know that whilst person might seem wonderfully friendly on the phone or on email, safety must come first.

That is the grim side of the coin, however, and for the most part, Craigslist reselling is a great opportunity to meet new people and learn about their lives and stories. You're basically getting socializing and business all rolled into one!

It's Good Fun

If you can create a way of working which is enjoyable, you'll find your reselling business to be quite fun. It will feel like more of a hobby than a job, and that's a great way to earn extra cash. It won't feel like work, because it's really not!

The crux of this point is that you need to ensure you organize your time well and that it doesn't become something you can't keep up with, or don't have the time for. Provided you do have the time and you do your research into what is going to work and what won't, you'll enjoy reselling on Craigslist, and it will create a fun sideline job for you.

It's a Way to Fill Your Spare Time

Look at it this way - you can either spend your spare time doing nothing constructive, perhaps even spending money you don't really have, or you can do something which is worthwhile and earns you some cash. Reselling on Craigslist is fun if you have the time, so if you are working part-time, or perhaps not working at all, you will find this to be a fun way to fill your spare time, and it will keep you away from other things which would cost money. Surely that's more useful?

Offers Freedom Away From The Office

If you can really make Craigslist reselling work for you, it will give you an official break from being stuck in an office. For those who manage to make a wage equivalent to that of a part-time job, you have total freedom to organize your time however you like. You are in effect your own boss and you don't have to answer to anyone.

If you have other demands on your time, e.g. a young family, you're caring for someone, or you have other responsibilities which you need to attend to, you can easily arrange your reselling endeavors around these things, without it becoming too much, or encroaching on the things you need to fit into your time.

In addition, you are not sat cooped up in an office, factory, or another working establishment, as you can work from anywhere, provided you have an Internet connection! You could even sit in your local cafe and work through your emails and list your new items.

Opportunities For Growth

If you organize your business well, there is a lot of room for growth here. You can start off with one item and see how that goes, monitoring sales and looking for trends. From there you can branch out into associated items, which are a little different but still have a link. A little earlier we mentioned selling cell phone cases and covers, and an associated product could be chargers or laptop cases, etc. There is a lot of scope for growth provided you do your research and learn which products are likely to sell well, versus the ones which won't.

These are the specific benefits of reselling on Craigslist, but you might even find a few more benefits that we haven't mentioned. You get out of it what you put in, and the more you focus your time, the more you will be able to make money-wise, and the greater enjoyment you will get out of your new endeavors. Look at it as a business and you'll focus your time and attention much more easily. Despite that, don't let it become a drag, and always keep enjoyment to the forefront of your mind. If you can do that, you'll win on all sides.

Chapter 2: What do You Need to Become a Reseller on Craigslist?

Now you know what reselling is, and you know what the benefits are, let's now talk about the things you'll need in order to make it all work.

There are six main elements you need to become a reseller on Craigslist, some physical and some more about mindset. Let's explore them in turn.

You Need a Computer/Tablet

These days you can do most things on a smartphone, but if you're going to be serious about making your reselling work for you, you should invest in a laptop, desktop, or at least a tablet. This will make it easier for you to look at prices, find items to sell, and list for yourself. You'll also be able to answer emails much more easily, and as a result, you won't miss any emails.

You can organize yourself much better on a computer, and if you want to keep your business ticking along, without receiving a bad reputation for not being up to date with communication, this is a vital part of the puzzle.

A laptop or tablet is probably preferable to a desktop PC because you have more freedom when you can move around. We mentioned earlier about doing some work from a coffee shop, or even in the park on a sunny day, and that is not at all possible with a large desktop computer! A laptop is ideal.

You Need a Reliable Internet Connection

You can't resell anything on Craigslist without an Internet connection, so make sure that you have WIFI or mobile Internet at the very least. You can easily set up a mobile Internet hotspot from your cell phone and use that, but you will be using your data. Again, coffee shops are ideal, because the WIFI is normally free!

You also need to be relatively free to answer emails when they come in, to avoid buyers waiting for too long for their answers. If you wait until the next day, they might have changed their mind and gone elsewhere. We're not suggesting you need to be connected 24/7, but the ability to check a few times a day is essential.

You Need a Phone

Buyers can decide whether to contact you via the telephone or via email. Some may prefer a more personal touch, and that way they can get their questions answered much quicker. For that reason, you need to have a cell phone which you can answer easily. Most people already have this, so it's not the biggest deal, but it is certainly something to bear in mind and consider.

Life Will be Easier if You Have a Car

Whilst it's not impossible to do your drop-offs without a car, you will find it much easier if you do. We are certainly not suggesting you go out to buy a car just for your reselling plans, but if you have one already, that is certainly going to make everything easier.

Craigslist is built on the idea that you are selling locally, and not having to send things via cargo or the regular post. This means the ability to meet people in mutually convenient places. Because you are providing a service, you should be able to reach most places in the local area, within reason. It's unreasonable to expect a buyer to travel a fair distance without transport when you are the one offering them the purchasing service. It is more towards the seller's side when it comes to how far to travel. Despite that, always remember safety.

There are going to be some items which simply cannot be taken to a place for collection, e.g. large items, but if you are going to specialize in large items, you need to come to an arrangement which is both safe and convenient for you in terms of pick-ups and drop offs.

A Passion For Searching For Great Deals on Craigslist or Elsewhere

You need to find the items you're going to resell somewhere and Craigslist is a great place to start! You can do these one of two ways. You can spend your time looking for real bargains on Craigslist and then resell them on when you receive them, or you can have a stock of items which you have sourced from elsewhere, e.g. trade sellers. It's up to you how you do it because both ways are classed as reselling.

Whichever option you go for, you need to dedicate yourself to finding those bargains to be able to resell on. We mentioned that reselling on Craigslist is a good passive income method, but it does require some work, and it isn't simply something which runs itself. If you can organize your time and enjoy looking for deals, you'll find it all much easier. If you hate searching for items to purchase and resell, you're not going to get optimum enjoyment out of your time and you're not going to find much pleasure in this business.

A Good Understanding of Market Prices

You also need to have a good understanding of how much things are selling for, and how low or high you can really go without your item being left unsold. This is something you will pick up much easier over time, but the first few times you need to be able to work with estimates. A good understanding of the market will help to establish your reselling efforts, so put some time into searching around on Craigslist for current listings, plus look at other sites, such as eBay, to give you another side of the coin.

If you list your items too high, nobody is going to buy them. If you list your items too low, you're not going to make a profit. Neither is a good option, and you need to find the necessary piece of positive middle ground. Research is the single best way to achieve that.

As you can see, you don't really need a whole lot to get started, but one thing we haven't mentioned is the items you want to sell! These will come to you as you get into the purchasing and reselling way of life. You are going to find items from other places, e.g. source items to resell on from wholesalers or other sellers, then you need to make sure that you establish positive and reliable relationships with those companies. You also need to make sure that you are certainly going to make a profit and sell the items, otherwise, you will be left out of pocket. Again, you'll know that by the market research you do.

Chapter 3: Reselling for Beginners

Now let's get practical!

You now know all the background information on reselling on Craigslist, but what you don't know yet is a step by step guide on how to source your first item and resell it. We are going to cover that in detail in our next chapter, but this chapter is going to give you plenty of hints and tips on what to do and what not to do. By avoiding pitfalls, you can create a much more likely to succeed picture.

We're going to assume that you're going to go down the easiest route of reselling, i.e. finding deals on Craigslist and selling them on. If you are going to source your items from elsewhere, the general way to do it will be the same, but you will need to find your items from the sources you find most reliable. That is something you will need to research and build up over time.

Stick to One Item First of All

It's best to stick to one item and not to overwhelm yourself with a million different items. If you do that you're not going to be sure who is calling or emailing about which item, and you're going to end up with more items than you know what to do with. This is when problems and mistakes happen. Stick to one item at a time and you will not only find it easier, but you'll also be able to minimize issues. As you become more experienced over time, you can try a few at one time, but for starters, stick to one niche and one item at a time.

For instance, if you are selling a Samsung cell phone, you would list that item, complete the process, field enquiries about it, and then hopefully sell it. You would then take it to the meeting place, swap the item for the cash, and then start your next cycle of searching for items and reselling. This is the single easiest way to start. Many people also choose to stick to this method, but if you want to add a few more into the mix as you become more experienced, that is something you will be able to do as confidence builds.

Also, Stick to One Group of Items

We talked earlier about finding out which items will sell well in your particular area and which don't have the greatest demand. It is best to stick to one particular niche, e.g. the cell phone case example we gave earlier. This will allow you to become an expert in that area, you'll understand market prices, and you then have scope for growth in the future.

If you start buying any old item, how can you be sure you're getting a good deal? You can't be an expert in all fields! You can branch out in the future, but for now, specializing is the best way forward. By becoming an expert in that particular area, you can see deals easier, you can sidestep issues easier, and you'll also find it much easier to make a profit overall.

Keep Accurate And Up-To-Date Records

It's impossible to be able to tell if something is working for you or not if you don't record things. By records, we are talking about keeping a note of how much you have bought and how much you have sold. This will help you identify if you need to cut back on your buying for a while until you've managed to sell a few items, or whether you can continue to search for deals. Basically, you can tell if you are breaking even, and how much of a profit is coming your way. If you're noticing less in the way of success, they can look to tweak how you are working and improve what you are doing.

These records don't need to be super in-depth, and they don't need to be official, just a list of things you've bought with a running total, versus the things you've sold. That will give you all the information you need. Keep it simple and don't overcomplicate matters.

Know Your Rights And The Rights of The Buyer

Craigslist doesn't tend to get involved in any sales unless there is a major dispute going on. The single best piece of advice is to solve any issues which arise between you and a buyer because if you don't, your reputation will basically go south. In this case, word will get around and you will not be able to sell as well in the future.

Again, think of your reselling hobby as a business. Every business needs to pay attention to its reputation and market its services in a positive way. Therefore, large businesses have dedicated customer services departments - because the customer needs to be listened to, and they need to have their grievances ironed out. If they don't, sales will be affected and therefore profits will be lower.

Never underestimate the power of the reputation in any part of life, especially when it comes to sales. Nobody is going to want to purchase items from someone who has a bad reputation, and who has been known in the past to not listen to their buyers, or not care about issues which arose. Nobody is going to care whether or not you were in the right or the buyer, they will simply see the issue and decide to go elsewhere.

Think about your own experiences with buyers, perhaps on eBay. If you saw that they had less than a perfect score, did you purchase from them? Probably not. If you did, you probably thought twice about it beforehand. Don't let that happen and simply communicate well and iron out any problems when they arise. It will be worth it in the long-run.

Safety Comes First

We mentioned this one previously, but it is so important that we need to highlight it again. Most people on this planet are honest, hard-working, and reliable people. Some, however, are not. You have no idea if the person you are meeting is in the latter or former category. Do not take risks. The best safety guidelines to follow are:

- Always meet in public places
- Always meet in daylight - midday and early afternoon are good times as there are more people around
- If the weather is bad and causing it to be dark and miserable, arrange for another time or meet somewhere indoors and public
- Cafes and restaurants are good places to meet, as are shopping malls
- If you feel nervous, make sure you take someone with you
- Never give a buyer your home address and ask them to come and pick up the item
- Never go to a buyer's address to drop an item off
- If for some reason you have no choice but to meet in a place which isn't as public as you would like, do not go alone - take someone you trust with you

It's common sense at the end of the day, but it can be easy to throw it out of the window and trust too easily. The kind and helpful person you are speaking to on the phone or via email may seem fine, but you do not know how they are in reality. The same advice goes for when you are purchasing items from Craigslist, in order to sell on.

Keep Reality in Your Mind When Looking For Deals

It can be very easy to let your mind run away with you and end up trying to buy items which in reality are not going to sell as well. Always keep your plan in mind and your common sense to the front of everything. At the end of the day, you are trying to make a profit, not a loss! As with our first point, stick to one niche which you know very well and you shouldn't go too far wrong.

Understand That it Might Take Time

It might not happen overnight for you, and you need to be fine with that fact. Miracles don't happen in seconds, remember! Persevere for a while, but if you find it isn't working, it could very well be that you simply need to change your niche or look at your pricing. There is no real reason why reselling items on Craigslist will fail, and if you're not making a profit, it's probably something quite easy which needs to be tweaked.

These are a few things you simply need to keep in mind when you start out on your reselling journey.

Chapter 4: The Five Important Tasks When Reselling on Craigslist

Reselling on Craigslist can easily be broken down into five easy tasks. It's that simple - just five tasks which you need to complete well, in order to find deals and sell them on for a profit.

We have broken it down into these easy steps because the whole process of reselling can seem quite overwhelming at first. This is simply because you are not familiar with it yet. Once you know what you're doing, it will seem like child's play.

The single best way to conduct reselling in the most efficient way is to research the process, familiarize yourself with it, practice once in a slow manner, and then ensure that you tie up any loose ends before moving forward with the next sale. When searching for deals, always make sure that you think twice before purchasing, and ask yourself whether it will make a realistic resale, for a good price.

This chapter is going to take you through the process of buying an item and reselling it, step by step. Print this chapter out and keep it as your guide throughout your first few attempts at reselling on Craigslist. After that, you'll be doing it with your eyes closed.

The process is:

1. Browse Craigslist to find deals and purchase the ones which make sense
2. Writing a quality advertisement for the item and reviewing it before posting
3. Taking quality pictures of the item, including any faults
4. Communicating with the person you are either buying or selling from
5. Driving or taking transportation to pick up the item

Of course, there are smaller tasks to complete the full step, but breaking it down into the smallest number of steps possible, makes the whole process less daunting.

Step 1 - Browse Craigslist to Find Deals

The first step is finding something to actually sell! At this point, you need to spend some time browsing Craigslist and looking for deals. The key point here is knowing the type of times you want to sell, i.e. your target niche. This will make finding deals easier because you can look in one or two categories, and not have to browse the entirety of the site.

Craigslist is arranged in product categories, e.g. jewelry, clothing, computer hardware, etc, and the list of categories is quite extensive. Before you begin looking for deals, deciding upon your niche is vital, if you want to be more time constructive. It will take you endless hours if you have no clue what types of things you want to resell because you'll have to look at everything. Do you know how many items are listed on Craigslist within one region every day? A lot!

Make your life easier and know what you want before you start.

From there, it's about browsing and knowing the market price. Again, this is something to research before you begin. It's a good idea to spend a few hours really digging into the ads which you see already listed and comprising prices. You could also do some cross-over work with eBay and other auction sites, to see if the same kind of marketing prices are evident. If not, you can see if the products already listed on Craigslist or too high, or too low, and come to the best price for you to buy the product and then ultimately resell it for. This will give you important information on how much you should offer because of course, you want to make a profit - that's the whole point!

Once you've found something you want to buy, reach out to the seller and make contact. You can do this either by email or telephone, whichever option they have mentioned on the ad, and whatever you are comfortable with too. Most people prefer telephone because it is more personal and much faster, but other people prefer emails because there is an electronic paper trail of evidence, so you can look back over what was said, where to meet, etc.

Only buy one item at a time at first. This will cut down on the chances of possibly losing out by making a profit margin loss, and will make life easier in terms of knowing which items are currently on your sales list.

It is perfectly acceptable to place an offer on the item and not offer to pay the full price, but do bear in mind that the person may say 'no'. For this reason, don't offer a wildly low price as you're simply going to insult them and they will not sell the item to you! A little lower than the asking price is sensible, and you can banter back and forth and reach an agreement from there.

Step 2 - Write a Quality Advertisement For Item You're Reselling

Now you have the item in your hands, you need to work to resell it. The first step is writing a quality advertisement and reviewing it, to check it includes all necessary details. It is best to cut down on the number of questions which buyers may ask you, to avoid everything becoming confusing and slow. The best way to do this is to anticipate questions and answer them in your ad.

As a bare minimum you should mention the following:

• The name of the item
• Specs, e.g. year, any functions or specific information related to the item
• Photos (more on that shortly)
• The price - it is always better to ask for more than you're willing to accept, but not wildly so. By doing this, you are giving yourself room for bartering, as buyers will always ask

to purchase for less. If you ask for more, you're not losing out on what you know you can get for the item
- A reason why you are selling
- A short description, which is concise and to the point

Your ad needs to be friendly but professional. Do not simply list features with bullet points and leave it at that, as this doesn't come over as particularly useful to buyers. Do not speak too much but simply be concise with the information the buyer needs to know. You should mention the reason for selling because it helps to build the bond of trust with the buyer. If they know you're simply selling it because you have no use for it anymore, they're more likely to be attracted to the item than if you don't mention it. In this case, they may think there is something wrong with it.

Always re-read your advertisement before posting it - bad grammar and spelling mistakes a very off-putting to many people!

Step 3 - Take Quality Photographs

This is a very important step. Make sure you take at least two quality photographs of the item and post them with your add. More than one photograph is always recommended because it gives the buyer more information. Obviously, you should take photos from different angles, to give the buyer a greater idea of what they are purchasing.

If there are any faults with the item, make sure you take photos of those too. You should also describe these in detail in your ad description - honestly is vital as your reputation will be damaged if you hide any important details.

Make sure the item is clean when you take the photos and that the background is clear, e.g. no items from your home that make the photo look unprofessional. It is best to move the item closer to a window or light in order to take the photo, as it will be clearer for the buyer to see the item up-close.

Step 4 - Communicating With The Buyer or Seller

At this point, you either want to buy an item, or someone has contacted you and is interested in purchasing the item you have listed. Either way, politeness and professionalism are vital.

You can either be contacted by email or telephone, and you should answer any queries you get as quickly as you can. This doesn't mean you need to answer every email within minutes, but it does mean checking your inbox a few times a day, to make sure you don't miss anything important. If you notice you have missed call on your phone, make sure you call them back as soon as it is convenient. Failure to do this potentially means a missed sale or purchase.

Make sure communication is clear. For instance, make sure you cover the basics:

- Answer any questions they have about the product
- Arrange the price
- Confirm that you will be receiving the money in cash, upon receipt of the item
- Arrange how you are going to get the item to them, e.g. arrange a mutually convenient meeting place in public, in daylight hours
- Confirm the drop once more before the arranged time

If there are any queries or concerns which happen after the sale, e.g. after you have taken the item to the person and they have paid you, make sure you iron these out as quickly as you can. Whilst the sale is officially over by this point, not answering someone's problems post-sale could land you with a poor reputation, as we explored in further detail a little easier on in the book.

Step 5 - Taking The Item to The Buyer/Picking up The Item

The rules for taking a sold item to a buyer, and picking up a deal you've found from a seller are the same. Safety is key!

Arrange a mutually convenient place to meet, and make sure that it is during daylight and in a public place. If you can meet somewhere like a shopping mall or a restaurant/coffee shop, this is going to be better than meeting on the street. We talked a lot earlier about safety, so simply heed these rules, but also make sure that the pickup or collection point is somewhere you can both easily reach.

Once more, it will be better if you have a car and your own transportation, however, if not you can use public transport, provided the item isn't too large.

This is the point where you hand over the cash, or the cash is handed to you. For buying and selling on Craigslist, payment by cash is always preferred. Never give your bank details to anyone, i.e. for them to put the money into your account. If the sale is for a large amount and cash simply isn't feasible, you can ask to use PayPal. This is a better option because you simply use the email address linked to your account, and you get a much safer experience as a result. Signing up for a PayPal account is also free, so if the buyer doesn't have one currently and the sale is for a large amount, it isn't too much of an issue to sign up and fix the transaction.

Once more - never give out your bank details and never use any third-party payment transaction other than PayPal. Cash is always the single best option.

And that is really it! That is your process of reselling on Craigslist, and as you can see, it's not a critically difficult process overall. For the first few times, it is going to take you longer because you need to gain experience of finding deals and also writing quality ads which are going to attract buyers to your items. Once you have more experience in doing that, you will find it faster and easier to list items.

Chapter 5: The Importance of Time Management & Planning

When you decide you are going to place effort and time into reselling on Craigslist, you need to organize yourself from the get-go. This will ensure that you overcome any hurdles faster, and hopefully, avoid them in the first place. It also means that you are much less likely to notice your reselling efforts encroaching on your own time and space.

First things first, how much do you want to make? Every business (and that's how you need to treat it) needs and aim. If you know a general amount of how much you want to recoup back, you'll be able to work towards that goal with more motivation than otherwise. Without an idea of how much you want to gain in profit, you're going to be bumbling around from sale to sale and not really noticing your gains.

Be realistic in this number, because at first, you might not notice the greatest profit coming your way. It may take time. Perhaps you will be lucky, i.e. you'll find some fantastic deals from the get-go and be able to rack up a tidy profit from your first few sales. It is possible, but it's always best to be realistic and aim for lower amounts, to begin with. Once your experience grows, you'll also notice your profits growing too.

We mentioned earlier that it is possible to make between $300 - 700 per month from reselling on Craigslist. For your first few months, perhaps aim for the $300 mark and see how you go. Make sure that you review your efforts as you move along and then give yourself a higher aim for the following month. This will push you to keep finding those deals and keeping selling items on. Before you know it, you'll be earning a part-time wage without even realizing it!

How to Manage Your Time Effectively

We've mentioned this phrase already, but the single best way to be organized and successful is to treat your reselling as a business. In many ways that is what it is. At its very core, business is something you spend time on and earn money from. That is what you are doing, so therefore you have a business!

At first, you need to do your homework and familiarize yourself with Craigslist, so it makes perfect sense that in the initial part, you're going to spend more time on your efforts. Once you purchase your first item and start reselling it is important to have boundaries. Do not dedicate your entire time to reselling on Craigslist. If you do that, and if you begin to treat it like a real job, you're not going to enjoy it. There is a difference between treating it as a business and treating it as a job. It should be a business you enjoy, not something you have to do otherwise you don't get paid!

Look at the time you have available and dedicate a set amount. Make sure that amount is reasonable, and that it isn't eating into all your spare time. Reselling on Craigslist shouldn't take too much of your time, and once you establish yourself and become more experienced, you'll notice that it takes an hour or two at the very most every day. On most days it will probably be even less.

It might be a good idea to note down how much time you are spending on it at first, so you can check that it isn't taking over your life. Time planning will help your reselling efforts remain enjoyable and profitable.

Keep Your Expectations Realistic

Of course, you want to make as much profit as you can, that is human nature and the very reason why you wanted to learn more about reselling on Craigslist, but you need to be realistic, otherwise you will fail from the start. You cannot buy something for $100 and expect to sell it on for three times that amount. Generally speaking, you can expect to make a profit of between 30-50% on the price you paid. That's not a bad amount!

There may be times when you grab a real bargain and resell it for a very tidy profit, but make peace with the fact that these occasions are likely to be very few and far between. If you keep your profit expectations realistic, you won't be disappointed and you will still line your profit coffers very handsomely.

By knowing what to expect when reselling on Craigslist, you will find it much easier to navigate your first sale. Information is power when it comes to dealing with sales and the public. Whilst most sellers and buyers you will come into contact with are honest and simply after a good price for an item they want, some may not be quite so honest. Being open to the fact that there may be scams here and there will help you know what to look for. A few red flags include:

- Unwillingness to speak on the phone, and only wants communication via email - This isn't always a sign of something amiss, but it can be in some circumstances
- Doesn't want to pay cash or use PayPal and tries to coerce you into payment via some other means
- You simply don't feel right about the transaction - sometimes listening to your gut is the best way forward
- They have bad feedback or a bad reputation in general

Listen to your inner voice and if something doesn't seem right, it's completely fine to pass on that sale or purchase and look for another. Your safety and your finances are not things you should gamble with. Overall, however, the overwhelming numbers of resales on Craigslist are easy, quick, and go without the slightest hitch.

Chapter 6: Secrets Tips to Boost Your Selling Power

We have gone through the process of reselling items on Craigslist and you now know the overall steps to take, but what about the hidden hints you can use to boost your selling power and ensure good quality and profitable sale?

Much of time, you will learn things as you go along, from experience, but it is also worth listening to advice from those in the know. Below you'll find a few secrets to help you make better sales, but remember to always follow the procedure through carefully, and to stick to the safety guidelines we talked about more than once in this book already. Those are the true basics, and any successful venture needs to have the basics covered carefully. After that, you can add boosts to give you a better experience and outcome.

Tip 1 - When Selling, Think Like a Buyer

You should never simply see your sales from a seller's point of view. Thinking like a buyer will help you to cover all bases and have a better selling outcome. For instance, why should they buy from you and not someone else? What makes you stand out? Why are you a better option? Make yourself stand out, give them something that nobody else does, e.g. high-quality customer service or a warranty after purchase. The small things make a huge difference and will help you to stand head and shoulders over your competition.

There are always going to be other sellers in the same niche as you, and they will be trying to outdo you at the same time. Thinking like a buyer will give you more information, and it will give you a different viewpoint on which to build your success.

Tip 2 - Cover All Bases in Your Advertisement

When writing your ad, make sure you have covered as much information as possible. Think about the questions buyers might ask, and thinking like a buyer (as in tip 1) will allow you to identify the things which might be asked of you. By doing this, you're cutting down on the time it takes for a sale to work, and it also makes the buyer trust you more, because you're knowledgeable and gives them what they need.

Think about times in the past when you have wanted to buy something. Of course, you wanted to find out the information you needed without having to ask a million questions. This simply looks more professional. You should also think about the time it takes for emails to ping back and forth with questions. Even phone calls can take time if you miss one or two at first.

Draft your advertisement first and then re-read it. You could even review it in line with another similar advert and see if you have covered the same bases, and then add extra information to make yourself stand out.

Tip 3 - Make Sure Your Photos Are High Quality

Check your photos before you upload them and look for any potential issues. For instance, is the item clean? Can you see items in the background that don't need to be there? Can you see the time clearly? Is the lighting sufficient? If you want to make a professional business out of your reselling endeavors, you need to make sure that the photos you show to people are equally as professional.

You don't need to purchase a specific quality camera to take these photos, as smartphones these days tend to have very quality picture taking facilities, but do make sure that the lighting is enough for the buyer to be able to check and really assess what they're buying. Remember, this isn't like in a shop when you can pick the item up and look at it for yourself. Whilst the buyer can ask to see the item when you go to meet to drop it off, by that point the sale is generally confirmed. Give the buyer all the visual information they need and you'll find more sales come your way as a result.

Tip 4 - Is The Sale Really Worth it?

Not every sale will be worth your time or effort. For instance, if someone from a rural area wants to purchase your item and it is going to take you far too long to get to the collection point and cost more in gas than the profit you're going to make, you need to think carefully about whether or not to proceed.

Reselling is not supposed to be a problem or a hindrance to your time, so if a sale looks like it is heading that way, you are within your rights to tell the buyer that you aren't willing to sell to them because of this very reason. Always tell them why, and don't leave it until the last minute, as that is common courtesy.

Your profit margin should be at least 20% from any sale you make, and that the lowest margin you should accept. Anything less than that and you are moving into territory which simply isn't worth your time or effort. At first, you might be worried about passing up sales, but doing so gives you the opportunity to make a more profitable sale in the near future.

Another thing to look at in terms of whether a sale is worth it or not is whether the profit margin is going to be enough. For instance, we just mentioned that the minimum 20% profit is what you should be looking for, but if you buy an item for $20, your 20% profit is only going to be $4. Is that worth your time? Probably not, but this is something to think carefully about, especially when searching for deals on Craigslist in the first place.

Tip 5 - Give Great Customer Service

People are much more likely to buy from you again if they had a good experience. Part of that is giving great customer service, even to those who simply contact you to ask a question about a product and don't actually end up buying it.

Always be friendly, always answer emails and calls, and always treat your buyers as you would want to be treated. Remember, you're treating your reselling as a business, and customer service is vital in any line of business.

We're not suggesting that you would be anything other than polite and friendly, but sometimes if you answer a call in a rush, e.g. you're in the supermarket and your phone rings, it's easy to be a little brusque. You certainly don't mean to be, but the buyer could take your attitude the wrong way and as a result, the sale doesn't go ahead. It's not this single sale that could be affected either, as in the future that person might see your name and not think to contact you about another item. They may even tell their friends not to buy from you. Remember, Craigslist is a local service, and word of mouth gets around very easily indeed.

Customer service is a very easy subject to cover, which makes it a no-brainer to tick it off your list. For instance, all you need to do is:

- Be professional
- Be friendly
- Be helpful
- Answer calls and emails
- Do what you promise you will do
- Be on time when you meet, and always be early if possible

It's that simple! It's about basic common courtesy, and if you can remember this whilst you're in the middle of trying to resell items and make cash, you'll find that more cash comes your way from sales overall.

Tip 6 - Build up a Bond of Trust With Your Buyers

Customer service and trust are two things which overlap, but trust is important enough to have a mention of its own. Your buyer needs to trust that you are giving them what they expect and that you are honest and open about the product. This is a baseline requirement and something you would expect from buying items from another seller yourself.

Again, look at this as a business. If you were to buy an item from a large supermarket, you automatically trust that you're getting what you pay for. This is because you trust that supermarket and you know that any problem you encounter would be sorted out quickly. This is the same kind of feel you're going for with your reselling efforts.

Building trust can take time, but it's not difficult. Giving great customer service is one way to go about this because you're instantly putting that person at ease. Feeling comfortable with a seller is one way for a buyer to feel that they trust you. There are a few other ways of doing this too:

- **Give your telephone number and not just your email** - Whilst it's completely acceptable to want to communicate solely by email, it does look a little 'off' in some ways. For instance, scammers will certainly not give out a telephone number and will only ever speak to potential buyers with email. Whilst you might have a completely honest reason for not wanting to give your telephone number out, the buyer may see it a different way. Be completely transparent and that trust bond will be easier to achieve.
- **Provide a small warranty if you are selling electronic items** - This isn't only limited to electronics, but this is the group of items which is probably the most risk-ridden. Electronics can break or go wrong at any time, and it probably has nothing to do with you or the way you handled it. To cut down on the risk and give your buyer more peace of mind, offer a warranty for one week after the sale. This will help them to see that there is nothing wrong with the item you're selling, and you're not hiding anything. The chances are the warranty will never be used, but the fact you're offering it looks positive.
- **Give a reason for selling in your advertisement** - Another way to help a buyer feel more comfortable and trusting, especially if you are selling electronics or large items, is to

give the reason why you are selling in your advertisement. If you don't do this, they might automatically think that there is something wrong with it, and you're trying to offload it for a profit. This isn't the case, so simply say that the item 'is in perfect condition, but is simply no longer used/no longer needed'. That is enough and is open and honest.

- **Always be friendly and professional** - The same as the customer service route, but being honest and open, professional and friendly shows the buyer that you are not scamming them, you are not hiding anything, and that they can trust your professionalism.

These are quick and easy tips you can use to boost your selling power and make your buyers feel more comfortable and at ease with your services. Remember, reputation is everything, and the better your reputation, the more likely you are to receive repeat sales in the future. Also, be sure to sort out any issues as they arise, and not to simply fly off the radar or not speak to the buyer once the sale has concluded. Most disputes are very easily sorted out and by doing so quickly, you're pleasing the buyer and ensuring that they will recommend you in the future.

Conclusion

And there we have it! You now know all there is to know about reselling on Craigslist and how to make a profit. When done correctly, reselling could certainly give you a substantial amount of spare cash every month. You could even decide to do this as a part-time job, alongside another job, or to bring extra cash to your bank account.

The hope is that by this point you're feeling much more relaxed about the process and more confident that you can make a success of this too. At first, it probably seemed like a mountain to deal with, but reselling is actually not that difficult. The key is finding deals to sell on in the first place, or sourcing goods from outside companies or manufacturers which you're sure you can resell for a good enough profit. Yes, it takes time at first, but as you become more experienced and more confident, you will find that you develop an instinct for a deal or bargain, and the selling side of things will become second nature.

This conclusion isn't the end of the story, however, as if you continue reading you'll find a bonus chapter, packed with information you can use to make your own business a major success. We've spoken to a successful power reseller in Vancouver, who has made a full-time job out of selling computer hardware. Through this Q&A session, you'll learn about how he started, how he built up his business, and how he runs it on a daily basis. Knowledge is power in this regard, and his huge success should be your inspiration!

Of course, we mentioned that it is entirely possible to make a part-time income of between $300 - 700 by reselling items on Craigslist, but it's not out of the question to push the bar further and make more. Our Q&A stands as a testament to that fact! Hopefully, you'll find plenty of inspiration to grow your own business.

There is one item we need to mention about once more, purely because of its sheer importance - safety.

Whenever you're dealing with the general public and people you don't know, you have to be on your guard, especially in this day and age. Whilst the vast majority of people you come into contact with will be completely honest and have good intentions, there are a very small minority of people who are simply trying to make a quick buck. You also have to be on your guard about general personal safety too, because you're going to be meeting these people in person.

Yet again - never visit a house or have anyone come to your home. If you have no choice, e.g. the item is so large it's impossible to take it to a mutual meeting place, make sure someone is home with you, or take a person to the buyer's home. It might sound like an overreaction and being very untrusting, but it's always better to be safe than sorry. Anyone buying an item from you will want the same kind of protection because safety works both ways. It's likely that if your buyer is a sensible person and you have to take the item to their home, they will also have someone at home with them because they don't know you too!

The vast majority of sales and purchases on Craigslist will be items which can be taken to a mutually convenient collection or drop off point. A few places which are ideal for meetings include shopping malls, restaurants, and coffee shops. If you don't want to hang around and you have other places to be, the inside of a shopping mall is a good idea. You could opt for just inside the main doors. The reason this is an ideal place is that it's easy to find, it's very public, and there are always security staff present in these places, especially in the doorways. That gives you peace of mind, and it ensures that the sale will go ahead safely. You can then go off and do your shopping with the extra cash!

Despite the safety concerns which have to be addressed, reselling on Craigslist is a fantastic way to make extra cash, and build a business which you enjoy. The more time you dedicate to your business, the more it will grow, and the faster too. Having said that, remember that this is also meant to be a side business which doesn't encroach completely on your time. Keep your time planning and management in hand and you'll have the best of both worlds.

Bonus Chapter – Interview with Albert in Vancouver, BC, Canada.

Full time reseller on Craigslist

How did you start your reselling business? And why?

Well, I didn't start reselling computer hardwares right away, I first started just selling stuff at home, like old cellphone, clothes, and just random stuff. The more I sell, the more I take it seriously, because you realized there are so many people browsing on Craigslist, everyone is different, but most people just want to get rid of the stuff they no longer need, so they price their item really low.

What do you find the hardest when selling on Craigslist?

Sometimes it is my English, because English is not my first language, so sometimes I misunderstand people, but most of the time, my English is enough for Reselling on Craigslist.

How much do you make a month for reselling?

To be very honest, from 1200-2500 if you are talking about just profit. On Monday to Thursday, there are less people browsing, but for Friday and Saturday, it can be crazy.

Do you think everyone can make money on craigslist?

Yes and No, and depending on what you are selling and where your location is. In Vancouver, there's quite a lot of people, so there are more money to be made. If you are in a small town, chances are there are much less people buying and selling.

How much time do you spend a day for the business?

Around 6-10, it depends sometimes. When I am not able to find any good deals, then I'll just skip a day and do something else, like listing or renew listings.

Do you people always pay what you ask for?

NO, people always want a lower price. Sometimes, for example you are listing something for 500, they will ask for 250?? You can pretty much expect different kinds of people buying your stuff. However, some people will just pay without negotiating at all. It all just depends on luck and timing. Don't get offended if people are lowballing you. You can just reply nicely saying no or give them another offer.

What is the most fun or enjoyable task when you are doing reselling?

I enjoy browsing on craigslist and just looking a deal , I can browse for 1-2 straight sometimes and it's fun when you are able to find a good deal. However, you need to be careful when something is too cheap. There might be problem with the item. It's always a good idea to check the item you buy in case of scam.

Why do you sell computer or computer hardwares?

Well, because I know how to build a computer and I know quite a lot in terms of how much a computer hardware worth. I do it 2 ways. Sometimes I will buy a computer and take everything out and sell it separately, but sometimes I buy different hardwares and put them all together and sell them as a whole PC.

What do you recommend doing if someone wants to sell computer and computer hardwares?

First, you need to know the price of all hardwares, you need to know how to put a PC together as well as how to separate the parts. I highly recommend learning from youtube videos, because nowadays, there are so many free video you can learn from. You also need to know the performance of the hardwares, especially CPUs and Video cards.

How many kinds of CPUs or Video cards there are?

1000ssss.. sometimes I don't know exactly how well a cpu or video card performs, I have to check on the internet.

What else do you think its profitable for reselling?

Books, video games and toys

What exactly do you do in your business?

A lot of different thing. I post new listing, browse for deals, negotiating with people, taking photo of items I list (good quality photo) and driving out to meet up.

What is the most important task when doing reselling?

Listing your ads correctly is the most important, because you can't price it too high or too low, your photo has to be clear, your ads has to be as professional as it can be, so people will trust you. People are skeptical, because they know they are buying used item, so be friendly and nice to build up trust.

Do you have some tips for people who just got started?

Yes, you need to know and understand the market for the item you are selling . Focus on a set of item, for example, maybe book. Then just sell books. Also, everyone should just start selling thing you no longer need, so you can just learn the process of reselling with no risk. Remember don't invite people to your home if possible. Always meet up at public place with a lot of people.

How much can you expect to make from each sale?

If I bought something for 100, I will need the item to sell for at least 130 to be profitable, because you have to list, meet up and resell, so it won't be worth it if I can't make at least 30% profit.

What is the most profitable item you sold?

A gaming pc, I remember buying a desktop PC for around 200$. I added a video card to make it into a gaming PC. I think I got 470$ profit from that flip. Just one flip. But of course, it's not easy to find this kind of deal. I would make around 150-250 problem selling gaming pcs.

Did you ever experience scam when buying from other people?

Most people are honest, I would say 95%. But Yes, I once bought a PC from someone, there are a lot of problem on that pc, the power button is not work, power supply has some problem and the ethernet card has some problem as well. At that time. I was just focusing on the spec of the PC and didn't check everything, so it's important to check before you buy.

Is driving important for reselling?

If you are doing reselling full time, yes. If not, you can sometimes ask the person to meet places close to you, but in many cases, people won't deliver for free

Last question, what are the advantage of reselling vs a traditional 9-5 job?

This really depends, and your personality, because when you have a job, it's stable and you get a paycheck every 2 weeks or a month, depending on where you live, but if you are doing reselling, income is not as stable. The good thing about reselling is that you can control your own time and not stuck at one place (eg in a warehouse or in an office). You get to meet different people and driving to different place.

For me, Reselling is a much more enjoyable comparing to a 9-5 job. That's for sure. I also enjoy building computer, so that is a win win.

The best thing to do is asking " Are you happy doing what you are doing? " If not, do something else and don't get trapped by your job just because you need the paycheck. Life is way too short.

Thank you for reading " The Advanced Craigslist Reselling Guide ".

*If you enjoyed this book and found this book helpful, please consider leaving a review, **even if it's only a few lines; it would make all the difference and would be very much appreciated. Thank you!***

Steve Johnson

www.ingramcontent.com/pod-product-compliance
Lightning Source LLC
Chambersburg PA
CBHW030736180526
45157CB00008BA/3192